BELONGS TO: ______________________________

Write Away Publishing

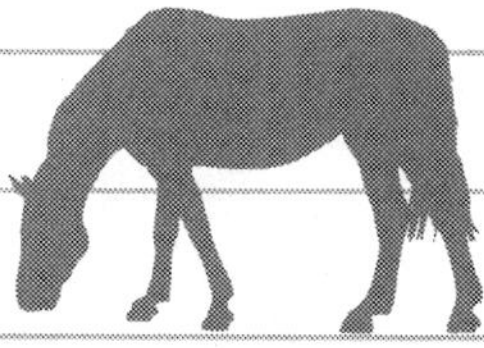

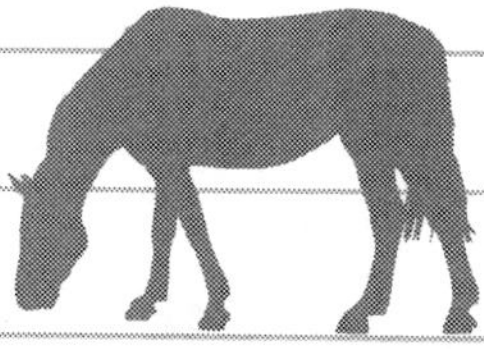

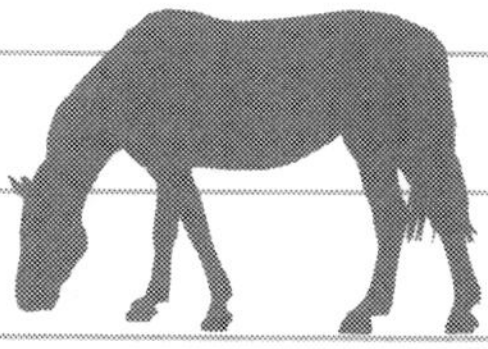

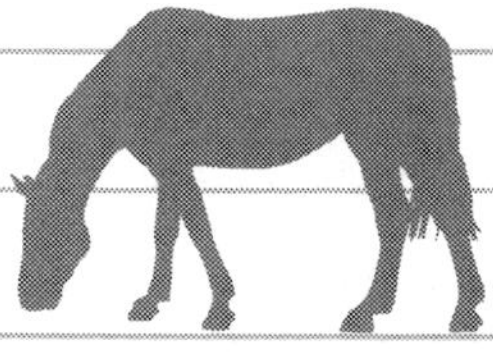

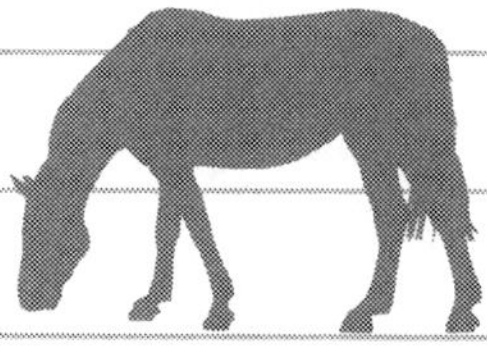

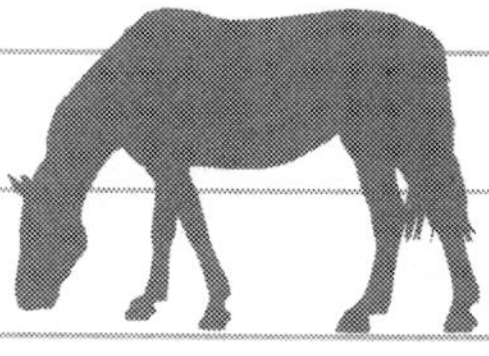

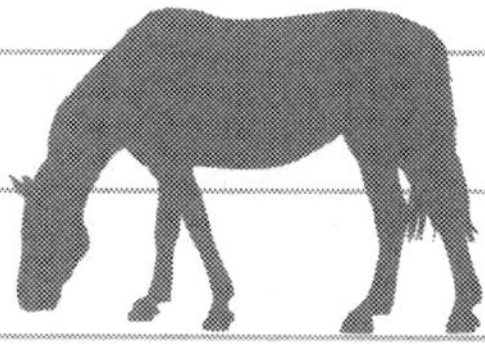

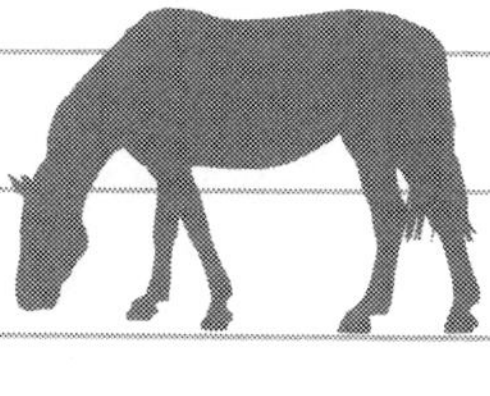

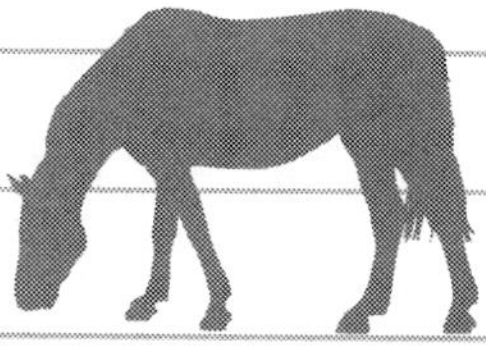

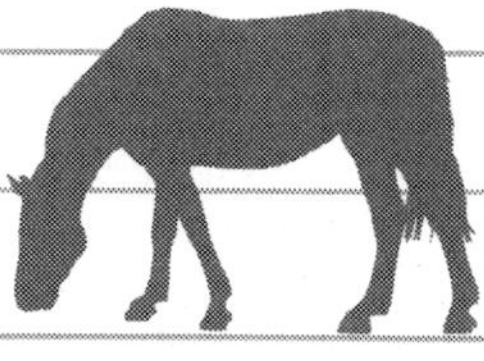

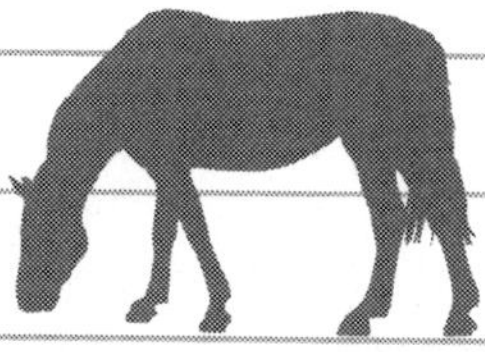

Made in the USA
Las Vegas, NV
31 August 2022

54454998R00068